THE AFRICAN CATS

Geoffrey C. Saign

A First Book

FRANKLIN WATTS
A Division of Grolier Publishing
New York • London • Hong Kong • Sydney
Danbury, Connecticut

For Rachael, Abby, Kassity, and Serena

Photographs©: Alan & Sandy Carey: 42, 45; American Museum of Natural History: 10; ENP Images: 29 (B. Castelein/BBC-NHU), 7, 26 (Gerry Ellis), 17 (Pete Oxford), 51 (Jagdeep Rajput), 5, 12, 13, 43, (Terry Whittaker); Kevin Schafer: 14, 22, 23, 40, 44, 49; Melissa Stewart: 36, 37; National Geographic Image Collection: 32 (Chris Johns); Photo Researchers: 48 (Gregory G. Dimijian), 30 (Clem Hagner); Tony Stone Images: 19 (J Sneesby/B Wilkins), 20 (Daniel J. Cox), 18 (Johnny Johnson), cover (Renee Lynn), 16 (Ian Murphy), 34 (Frank Lane/Parfitt), 39 (Mark Peterson), 47, 53 (Art Wolfe); Visuals Unlimited: 25 (Ken Lucas), 33 (Kjell Sandved).

Illustrations by Greg Harris

Visit Franklin Watts on the Internet at:
http://publishing.grolier.com

Library of Congress Cataloging-in-Publication Data

Saign, Geoffrey C.
    The African cats / Geoffrey C. Saign.
        p. cm. (A First Book)
    Includes bibliographical references and index.
    Summary: Describes the physical characteristics and behavior patterns of cats found in Africa.
    ISBN 0-531-20365-4 ISBN 0-531-15955-8 (pbk.)
    1. Felidae—Juvenile literature. [1. Felidae. 2. Cats. 3. Zoology—Africa.]
I. Title. II. Series.
    QL737.C23S225 1999
    599.75'096—dc21   97-41629
                                                                        CIP
                                                                         AC

©1999 by Geoffrey C. Saign
All rights reserved. Published simultaneously in Canada.
Printed in the United States of America.
1 2 3 4 5 6 7 8 9 10 R 08 07 06 05 04 03 02 01 00 99

GROLIER
PUBLISHING

CONTENTS

INTRODUCTION

A house cat is sitting on the windowsill of a seventh-floor apartment. It sees a pigeon fly by. The impulse to catch the bird is so strong that the cat leaps out of the open window. As it falls toward the ground, the cat first twists its head, and then its back until its feet are positioned below its body. Even though the cat continues to fall, its body is relaxed. Unbelievably, when it hits the hard pavement, the cat's legs absorb the impact and the animal is not injured.

Some people might say the cat survived "because it has nine lives." But cats don't really have nine lives; that's just a *superstition*. The cat lived because it has an amazing ability—it can *orient* its body in midair. Humans do not have this ability.

If the cat had been closer to the ground—on the first or second floor, for example—it probably would have been hurt. It wouldn't have had enough time to position its body properly and then relax before it hit the ground.

The cats we keep as pets are one type of small cat. Other small cats include caracals, servals, African gold-

Because all modern house cats descended from the African wildcat, they have many of the same physical traits and abilities as wild cats.

en cats, African wildcats, black-footed cats, jungle cats, African wildcats, and sand cats. These small cats are closely related to big cats such as tigers, lions, leopards, and jaguars. Cats can be found in North America, South America, Europe, Asia, and Africa. Ten types of cats are found primarily in Africa. Some prefer the open plains of the savanna, while others live in lush tropical rain forests. The African cats include the fastest land animal and the *ancestor* of all modern house cats.

COMPARING AFRICAN CATS

African Cat		Body Size
Lion		Weighs 300 to 500 pounds (135 to 225 kg); 9 to 11 feet (2.7 to 3.3 m) long
Leopard		Weighs 130 to 160 pounds (58 to 73 kg); about 8 feet (2.5 m) long
Cheetah		Weighs 80 to 140 pounds (36 to 63 kg); about to 7 feet (2.1 m) long
Caracal		Weighs 22 to 40 pounds (10 to 18 kg); about 61 inches (155 cm) long
Serval		Weighs 20 to 40 pounds (9 to 18 kg); about 48 inches (120 cm) long
African golden cat		Weighs 24 to 31 pounds (11 to 14 kg); about 57 inches (145 cm) long
African wildcat		Weighs 7 to 18 pounds (3.2 to 8 kg); about 46 inches (117 cm) long
Black-footed cat		Weighs 2.2 to 5 pounds (1 to 2.3 kg); about 22 inches (56 cm) long
Jungle cat		Weighs 10 to 30 pounds (4.5 to 13.5 kg); about 48 inches (122 cm) long
Sand cat		Weighs 4 to 8 pounds (1.8 to 3.6 kg); about 36 inches (91 cm) long

tures/Behavior

est African cat; most social wild cat; lives in a *pride*; largest eyes of any carnivore; cat with tufted tail and mane; prefers to eat *ungulates*, but will eat any animal

secretive cat; skilled stalker; extremely powerful; lives in rain forest and *arid* rt habitats; often hunts from trees; prefers medium-sized ungulates, but will eat small animal—even insects; can live close to humans

est land animal, can run 70 mph (110 km/hr); hunts mainly by sight; has hard pads like a dog; claws are only partially *retractile*; most gentle and shy wild cat; ot defend itself very well; eats small ungulates, birds, hares, and lizards

called the desert lynx; extremely acrobatic; fastest cat of its size; barks loudly to other caracals; eats impala, dik-diks, lizards, birds, and insects

enormous ears, long legs, and short tail; hunts by sound in tall grass; pounces rey with graceful, bounding leaps; eats hares, birds, fish, lizards, rodents, frogs, insects

ed tree climber; lives in the rain forest; often nocturnal; shy; eats rodents, birds, small ungulates

estor of common house cat; honored in ancient Egypt; eats birds, rodents, ds, snakes, and insects

called the anthill tiger; smallest African cat; black hair on bottom of feet; skilled er; very aggressive when threatened; eats rodents, birds, lizards, eggs, spiders, insects

ge, tufted ears; sphinxlike appearance; honored in ancient Egypt; eats rodents, ds, frogs, fish, insects, and young ungulates

s in desert regions; has big ears and furry footpads; barks like a dog at night; r climber and jumper; excellent digger; eats *jerboas*, hares, birds, lizards, es, and insects

Some scientists think that dinictis is the ancestor of all wild cats.

Chapter 1
WHAT IS A CAT?

About 65 million years ago, the dinosaurs suddenly began to die out. Their disappearance allowed a small, tree-dwelling animal called the *miacid* to develop. About 40 million years ago, some of these early meat-eaters began to live on the ground. These miacids became the ancestors of all *carnivores*. Today, there are nine types of carnivores: dogs, civets and mongooses, raccoons, bears, hyenas, weasels, eared seals, earless seals, and cats.

According to some scientists, the first true cat was a North American animal called dinictis. Scientists believe it looked like an overgrown house cat. At some point, dinictis split into two separate groups. Today, we call one group the Machairodontinae (the stabbing cats) and the other group the Felidae (the biting cats). At one time, the Machairodontinae included four different types of sabertoothed tigers. The last saber-toothed tigers died out about 10,000 years ago.

All modern cats descended from the Felidae. As time passed, the Felidae evolved into three distinct groups—small cats, big cats, and cheetahs. There are thirty-five kinds of cats alive today. Although each type of cat has

11

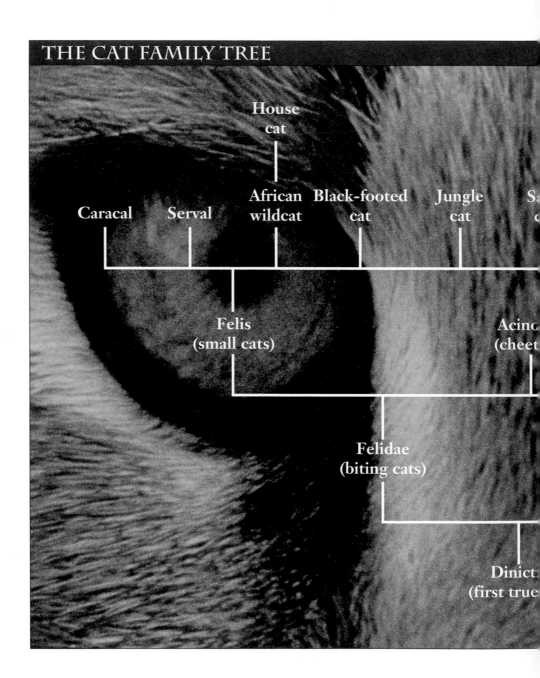

House
cat

Caracal   Serval   African   Black-footed   Jungle   S:
wildcat   cat   cat   c

Felis
(small cats)

Acino
(cheet

Felidae
(biting cats)

Dinict
(first true

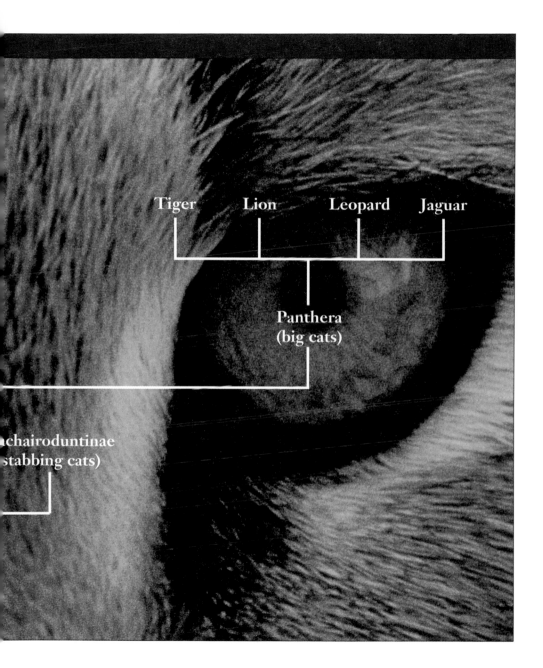

Tiger   Lion   Leopard   Jaguar

Panthera
(big cats)

chairoduntinae
stabbing cats)

Cats are excellent night hunters. In the dark, they can see six times better than humans.

adapted specific features that help it survive in its habitat, all cats have a great deal in common.

For example, all cats are excellent hunters. Because most hunt at night, their eyes have a special layer of tissue called the *tapetum lucidum* behind the retina. In dim light, the tapetum lucidum reflects light back through the retina like a mirror. This special feature allows cats to see six times better than humans in the dark. While the big cats have round pupils, small cats have vertical slits for pupils. The large, rotating ears of all cats allow them to hear better than most other animals.

All cats have spotted or striped fur that helps them blend in with their surroundings. Because they have soft footpads, they can sneak quietly through the grass or jungle as they stalk prey. Their flexible spines and strong muscles give them the ability to pounce on potential victims with all their weight. A cat's long tail helps it balance as it runs.

Have you ever watched a cat walk? All cats are called *digitigrades*—they walk on their toes rather than on the flat part of their feet. In fact, the heels of most cats are actually several inches above the ground when they walk.

At the tip of each toe is a claw. Cats have the ability to retract, or pull in, their claws. They extend their claws only when they are attacking prey or feel threatened. Because the claws do not touch the ground when a cat walks or runs, they do not often break off. Cats keep their claws razor sharp by scraping them against tree trunks. Some cats use their *dewclaw*, the first claw on their front paws, to drag down prey and climb trees.

While small cats must feed several times each day, large cats can survive for several days without hunting because they attack larger victims. Cats do not need to drink water very often. They get most of the water they need from their prey. When cats are not hunting, they spend most of their time resting or sleeping.

Cats use tail movements, body expressions, facial expressions, and sounds to communicate with one another. As cats move from place to place, they urinate on rocks, trees, and bushes. When another cat passes by, it can detect special chemicals in the urine. Cats have an excellent sense of smell.

Cats use their powerful canine teeth, or fangs, to kill prey.
Their side teeth, call carnassials, are used to shear meat off prey.

When a cat attacks a victim, it uses its *canine* teeth to bite the animal's throat. This kills the prey instantly. The cat then uses its side teeth, called *carnassials*, to shear off chunks of meat. A cat's tongue is covered with *papillae*—small hooklike projections that can tear meat right off bones. Cats swallow meat without chewing it; their digestive system can break down the large chunks.

Some cats have tiny facial scent glands. By rubbing their faces and bodies on objects, they leave scents that help them attract and find mates. On the roof of a cat's mouth, just behind the front teeth, is a *vomeronasal organ* that allows it to smell and taste the scents of other cats. When a male cat smells a female's scent, he wrinkles his nose, curls his upper lip, and opens his mouth—a behavior called the Flehmen response.

Cats make a variety of sounds. All big cats can roar. They have a specialized *hyoid bone* that causes them to purr when they breathe out. Small cats can't roar, but they can meow and purr. Cheetahs cannot roar either, but they can chirp and purr loudly. Some cats make barking sounds. The sounds that cats make can be used to judge their moods or intentions.

Most cats have a territory—a specific area in which they hunt for food, search for mates, and raise young. Each cat uses scents to mark the borders of its territory. It may also scratch

Cats often use sounds to communicate. This cheetah mother is calling her cubs with soft chirps.

This fallen tree is within the territory of these female lions.

Lions and other big cats have one litter every 2 years.
Many of the cubs are killed by predators or other lions.

trees and the ground to warn other cats of its presence. If another cat invades its territory, a fight may begin. In some cases, one cat will be killed.

All cats are *polygamous*. The male usually leaves the female right after mating. Big cats usually have one litter every 2 years, while small cats may produce one or two litters each year. Cubs or kittens are born blind and helpless. The young cats begin to learn hunting and fighting skills through affectionate play with the mother cat.

*Lions are the biggest African cat. Adult males have shaggy
manes that make them look even bigger, and protect them
during fights with other males.*

Chapter 2
THE LION

You know what a lion looks like—a big, powerful beast covered with golden-yellow fur. The fur on a lion's back is a little darker than the fur on its sides, and its belly and neck are even lighter. A lion's long tail has a black tassel at the tip. An adult male has a large shaggy mane around its head and neck. The mane protects the lion from injury during fights and makes him look even larger and more ferocious.

Lions are the largest African cat—only the tigers of Asia are larger. Adult males weigh up to 500 pounds (225 kg). They can be 11 feet (3.3 m) long and their shoulder height is usually about 3 feet (1 m). Adult females are smaller.

Lions are the most social wild cat. They live in groups called prides. A pride usually consists of one to six males, four to twelve females—called lionesses—and several cubs. When two lions from a pride meet, they rub against one another, lick each other, hold their tails high, and purr.

Because the lions in a pride hunt as a team, they are able to attack larger animals than a lion hunting alone.

When lions from the same pride meet, they often
lick each other and purr.

They are also better able to protect their kills from hyenas or jackals.

Each lioness nurses and protects all the cubs in the pride. The males patrol the pride's territory and protect the group from other male lions and hyenas. Lions announce their presence in an area by spraying territorial urine scents and roaring each morning and evening. A lion's roar can often be heard 5 miles (8 km) away. Lions also cough, growl, or snarl when they are angry.

While female lions often live more than 16 years, males rarely live more than 12 years. Many are killed in fights with outside males. When a pride's males are killed or driven away, new males join the pride and kill all the cubs. The new males do not want to invest energy raising the cubs of other lions. If a lioness has no cubs to raise, she will be ready to mate with a new male sooner.

Females begin mating when they are about 3½ or 4 years old. During a lion's 5 to 7 day mating period, the animal does not eat. Females have a litter of up to four cubs every 2 years. The cubs are born about 3½ months after mating. In most cases, all the females in a pride give birth within a few days of one another.

Lion cubs remain in the den for the first 6 weeks of their lives. Then, the mother returns to the pride, bringing the cubs with her. Cubs begin to hunt when they are 3 months old and weigh about 100 pounds (45 kg) by the time they are 1 year old.

Lion mothers keep their cubs away from the pride for 6 weeks. Cubs can begin to hunt when they are about 3 months old.

A female remains in her mother's pride for her entire life. Males, however, are forced out of the pride when they are 2 to 4 years old. In most cases, the male cubs stay together and are *nomadic* for 2 or 3 years. When the males are 5 or 6 years old, they begin looking for a pride of their own.

According to ancient records, lions once lived throughout Europe, China, India, Siberia, and North America. The Greeks were the first to describe them; the Romans forced them to fight gladiators in public arenas; and ancient Europeans painted them in caves. While lions no longer live in Europe or most parts of Asia, they can still be found in Africa. A few also live in the Gir Forest of India.

Lions live in all types of environments—sparse forests, vast grasslands, dry deserts, and mountains more than 3 miles (4.8 km) above sea level. Although lions typically spend 18 to 20 hours a day sleeping, they may walk up to 4 miles (6.4 km) searching for food and water. Most of the hunting is done by the females. As they move through the tall grass, they hold their tails high so that each lioness always knows the position of the others.

When the lionesses are close to their prey, some crouch low in the grass while the rest move around to the other side of the potential victim and hide in the underbrush. The crouching lions begin to edge closer.

The Asiatic lion lives in the Gir Forest of India.

When the prey senses the lions sneaking toward them, it turns and runs—toward the lions hiding in the underbrush. These lions leap out and ambush the prey.

If the prey somehow manages to avoid the lions' trap, it must still outrun the lions. A lion can run 35 mph (56 km/hr) for short distances. In addition, it can jump up to 35 feet (11 m), swim, and climb trees.

A lioness can easily knock down a 400-pound (180-kg) zebra with its front legs and drag the animal until it falls over. To kill its prey, the lioness bites its victim's neck or throat. A hunting lioness is successful about 25 percent of the time.

Lions eat their prey where it falls. Males eat first, then females. Cubs eat last. If there is little meat, the cubs may starve. Lions eat up to 50 pounds (22.5 kg) of meat at one time. Their sharp tongue papillae allow them to lick the meat right off the bones.

Lions prefer wildebeest and zebra, but they will eat

These lionesses are eating wildebeest, one of their favorite meals.

almost any animal—including fish, birds, snakes, warthogs, crocodiles, and rodents. Lions are also *scavengers*. If they have the chance, they will steal a kill from a hyena, a leopard, or a cheetah.

Lions may be known as the "kings of the jungle," but they run away from elephants, rhinos, and hyenas. A pack of hyenas can kill an adult lion.

Chapter 3

THE LEOPARD

The leopard is a solitary creature. It is unusual to see two or more leopards together, unless they are a mating pair or a mother with young cubs. Adult leopards avoid each other by scent-marking their territories and scratching trees.

After scent-marking an area, a leopard usually makes harsh coughing or rasping sounds. If two leopards do happen to meet, they often make a "woofing" sound to show their surprise. Then they growl, hiss, and snarl at each other. A leopard makes these same noises when it encounters an enemy, such as a lion, a hyena, a crocodile, or a troop of baboons. Leopards try to avoid their predators by hunting at night.

Leopards are the smallest of the big cats. They have yellow or reddish-brown fur with black spots. Their undersides are white. Some jungle leopards—called black panthers—are pure black. Male leopards weigh about 130 pounds (58 kg). They are about 8 feet (2.5 m) long, standing 2.3 feet (0.7 m) at the shoulder. Females are slightly smaller. All leopards are stocky and amazingly strong. They have powerful jaws, a massive skull, and a long tail.

Leopards are usually solitary. They spend most of their time in trees—hunting, resting, or eating prey.

Leopards have successfully adapted to more habitats than any other wild cat. They are found in Africa, the Middle East, central Asia, and on the islands of Borneo, Sumatra, and Java.

The leopard's favorite prey is a group of animals called ungulates. This group includes impala, hartebeest, wildebeest, and gazelles. But if ungulates are hard to find, a leopard will eat a variety of other animals—baboons, cheetahs, lion cubs, hyenas, birds, reptiles,

Leopards excellent stalkers. They prefer to eat ungulates, such as this Thompson's gazelle.

amphibians, and even insects. It also scavenges for prey killed by other carnivores. The leopard's flexible diet, along with its ability to climb and swim, allows this big cat to live successfully in a many different habitats.

Unlike most other cats, leopards are not afraid to live near humans. When humans are within their range, leopards hunt only at night, and may eat a farmer's livestock or dogs. The greatest danger of living near humans is the possibility of being trapped. In many parts of the world, leopards are still killed for their beautiful fur.

The leopard is an excellent hunter because it is intelligent, quick, and determined. A leopard may stalk an animal for nearly 2 miles (3.2 km), inching along almost on its belly! When it gets close enough, it leaps forward and knocks the prey down with its massive front legs. The leopard kills its victim by biting its neck or throat. A leopard's hunt is successful about 8 percent of the time, and it is more likely to catch prey at night.

Leopards like to sleep and rest in trees. In fact, they spend more time in trees than any other big cat. They often hide their kill from scavengers by hanging it on high tree branches. One leopard, for instance, was seen dragging a 300-pound (135-kg) giraffe for 1 mile (1.6 km), and then pulling it up into a tree for safekeeping.

These big cats remain near a kill and return to eat from it several times. On average, they kill one large ani-

A leopard hauls the carcass of an impala into a tree,
so other predators will not steal the kill.

mal each week, and may eat smaller prey in between. A leopard needs at least 50 pounds (22.5 kg) of meat a week.

A leopard spends most of the day napping. Sometimes it hunts or patrols its territory. The territory of a male leopard usually overlaps the territories of several females. Only that male leopard mates with the females in its territory.

A female leopard begins mating with males when it is 3 years old. Most females mate with older dominant males. The pair stays together for about 5 days, then the male leaves. About 3 months later, the female gives birth. A female has a litter of up to four cubs every other year.

Leopard cubs live with their mother for about 2 years.
Then they leave and look for their own territory.

A mother leopard is very protective of her cubs. She moves them from place to place to hide them from predators, but the cubs are often attacked when the mother leaves to hunt for food. In many cases, only one cub survives to adulthood. In their natural habitat, leopards generally live for no more than 15 years, but they may survive for up to 20 years in *captivity*.

Cubs nurse for 3 months. Then, the mother takes them to kill sites and lets them feed on meat. Most leopards make their first kill when they are about 1 year old. When a cub is about 2 years old, it leaves its mother and looks for its own territory.

*The flexible shoulders and spine of the cheetah allows it to run
faster than any other mammal alive today.*

Chapter 4
THE CHEETAH

Cheetahs are legendary for their speed. They can run close to 70 mph (110 km/hr) and can go from 0 to 45 mph (72 km/hr) in just 2 seconds! These graceful animals can reach such tremendous speeds because their flexible shoulders and spines stretch out more than those of other animals. This gives them a running stride of 20 feet (6.1 m). Their long legs also help them run faster.

Cheetahs have partially retractile claws, but there is no skin sheath over their claw tips. As a result, they have duller claws than other cats. Their dull claws and hard footpads help them gain traction when running.

The cheetah weighs up to 140 pounds (63 kg). It is about 7 feet (2.1 m) long, with a shoulder height of 29 inches (74 cm). It has a small round head, powerful chest, lean body, and long tail. Unlike lions and leopards, cheetahs cannot roar, but they can mew, yelp like a dog, and purr—especially when grooming each other.

The name "cheetah" comes from the Hindu word "chita," which means "spotted one." This big cat has a coarse coat of yellowish-gold or reddish hair broken up by black spots. Its underparts are whitish and its tail has three to six black rings near the white tip at the end. A

Cheetahs often sit on rocks or termite mounds and look for prey.

distinctive black stripe runs from the inside corner of each eye to the corner of the mouth. The spots of some African cheetahs blend into lines and blotches, giving the cat a beautiful coat.

Cheetahs prefer grassy plains, open woodlands, and *semideserts*. At one time, they could be found in Asia, the Middle East, and Russia. Today, small groups live in central and South Africa. A very small number may live in Iran and Egypt.

Cheetahs are gentle, shy, and easy to tame and train. Egyptian pharaohs and Sumerians once kept them as pets. Russian, Indian, French, and Arabian rulers trained cheetahs as hunting pets, called coursers. Akbar the Great, a Mogul emperor, is said to have kept 1,000 Asian cheetahs.

After killing their prey, cheetahs must often rest before eating. Then they eat quickly, before other predators try to steal their meal.

Because the cheetah hunts mainly by sight, it is active in the early morning and late afternoon. During these periods, the hot sun is not so bright. When a cheetah hunts, it sits atop a rock or termite mound and scans the area for prey. As soon as it spots a likely meal, it glides slowly through the tall grass toward the grazing animal. Whenever the unsuspecting victim raises its head, the cheetah freezes. The cheetah's coloring makes it difficult to spot among the tall grass.

When the cheetah is within 100 feet (30 m) of its target, it bursts forward at full speed and trips the prey with its dewclaw or swipes its paws at the animal. The cheetah kills the animal quickly by strangling it with a bite to the throat.

A cheetah's success rate is about 50 percent—considerably higher than the kill rate of lions or leopards. Cheetahs eat about 5 pounds (2.3 kg) of meat a day. Their favorite prey include Thomson's gazelles, impalas, and other ungulates, but they also eat livestock, birds, hares, and lizards.

Cheetahs can sprint for only 20 to 60 seconds. They are so winded by the chase that they must rest for up to 30 minutes before they can eat. Then the cheetahs feed as quickly as they can. They know that other predators—lions, packs of wild dogs, leopards, vultures, or hyenas—will soon arrive.

Lions and leopards often kill cheetahs for their prey. A cheetah cannot defend itself against these cats because its body is weaker and its claws are duller. The cheetah must surrender its kill to these predators, so it never has the opportunity to feed on the same kill twice.

Adult females begin to mate when they are 2 years old. Males do not mate until they are slightly older. A mating pair spends several days together, then the male leaves. About 3 months later, the female gives birth to three to six cubs.

The cubs have dark bellies and a mantle of silver-gray fur on their backs. This coloring helps them hide from potential predators. Even though the mother cheetah moves her young often, it is not unusual for lions, hyenas, jackals, and large birds to kill the cubs while the mother is hunting.

*To hide young cheetahs from predators, their mothers
guard them carefully and move them often.*

The cubs' coloring begins to change when they are
about 3 months old. By this time, they can outrun most
predators and are old enough to follow their mother as
she hunts. After the mother makes a kill, she calls her
cubs with a chirping sound. When the cubs are about
1 year old, they begin to hunt with their mother.

Cubs usually leave their mother by the time they are
1½ years old. In most cases, the cubs stay together for at

least 6 months. They hunt together and protect one another from lions and hyenas. Then, the female cubs establish territories that overlap with their mother's.

More than half of all male cheetahs form *coalitions*—groups of two to four related males. Research has shown that cheetahs in coalitions live longer, healthier lives than solitary males. Male cheetahs defend a 15-square-mile (39-sq-km) territory, which is scent-marked with urine. A coalition of males will kill any solitary male that invades the territory. Cheetahs are usually somewhat nomadic within their territory because they follow migrating herds of prey animals.

Male cheetahs often live and hunt in groups called coalitions. The members of a coalition are usually brothers.

40

Chapter 5

CARACALS AND SERVALS

THE CARACAL

Caracals are small, reddish-brown animals that weigh up to 40 pounds (18 kg). They stand about 20 inches (51 cm) tall and are about 61 inches (155 cm) long. The caracal's most notable features are the long tufts of black hair on its ears. In Turkish, *karakul* means "black ears."

The caracal is so fast and acrobatic that it can knock down a dozen pigeons in a single leap! It hunts only at night, and may travel 12.5 miles (20 km) searching for prey, such as birds, rodents, reptiles, insects, hyraxes, reedbucks, dik-diks, and impalas.

When a caracal spots a potential meal, it crouches low and stalks the animal. At the last moment, the caracal sprints toward its target, leaps into the air, and swats the prey with all its strength. When the victim falls, the caracal pounces on it and swats it again and again. The caracal then kills its stunned victim by biting its neck. This hunting technique ensures that the caracal is not injured by its prey. If the kill is a large animal, the caracal tries to hide it from other carnivores and returns to feed on it for several days.

Caracals have long tufts of black hair on the tips of their large ears.

Caracals, which are also known as desert lynxes, are found on savannas, in dry woodlands, and in hilly areas. Not all caracals live in central and southern Africa. They can also be found in southern Asia and the Middle East.

Caracals begin to mate when they are about 1 year old. About 2½ months after mating, a female gives birth

Female caracals nurse their kittens for 10 weeks. The kittens stay with their mother for about 1 year.

to a litter of up to four kittens. Female caracals nurse their kittens for about 10 weeks. The young caracals stay with their mother for about 1 year. Caracals live for up to 19 years in captivity.

Most males have territories between 12 and 25 square miles (31 and 65 sq km) in area. Several smaller female territories lie within each male territory. Caracals living in the same region use loud barking calls to communicate with one another. They growl and spit at enemies.

THE SERVAL

Although most servals have golden fur marked with black dots and stripes, some are pure black. The name

43

Servals have very beautiful fur and large ears.

"serval" comes from a Portuguese word that means "wolf deer."

Servals weigh up to 40 pounds (18 kg). They are about 26 inches (66 cm) tall and 48 inches (120 cm) long. These cats have small heads, short tails, large oval ears, and very long legs. Their forelegs are so long that servals have to lie with their legs out-stretched like a dog.

Servals live in grass-lands, scrub country, wetlands, and woodlands. Their primary predators are leopards, wild dogs, and humans. They are sometimes hunted for their fur or for food. Farmers may also kill servals to protect their livestock.

Besides livestock, the serval eats low-flying birds, hares, rats, mice, insects, frogs, lizards, and fish. An adult serval may eat up to 4,000 rodents a year, hunting mainly in the early morning and late afternoon. When it is stalking its prey through tall grass, it relies com-pletely on sound. As soon as the serval detects the

This serval is listening to the movements of a potential victim.

slightest movement, it leaps as high as it can and pounces on its prey. Like the caracal, the serval swats its prey until the victim is senseless, and then kills it with a well-placed bite. The serval is a successful hunter about 50 percent of the time.

A serval begins to mate when it is about 2 years old. About 2½ months later, the female gives birth to a litter of one to four kittens. The young servals nurse for about 3 weeks, and then begin to eat meat. By the time they are 8 months old, the kittens are able to hunt on their own. Like caracals, servals live for up to 19 years in captivity.

Chapter 6

MORE SMALL CATS

THE AFRICAN GOLDEN CAT

African golden cats have gold to orange fur with black or gray spots and whitish underparts. They have rounded ears. Adults weigh up to 31 pounds (14 kg). They are 20 inches (51 cm) tall and about 57 inches (145 cm) long.

African golden cats live in the rain forests of western and central Africa. They are usually found in areas with dense vegetation and an adequate supply of water. They

African golden cats are shy, and are only found in areas with dense vegetation.

46

often live in the same regions as leopards, but they eat smaller prey—rodents, birds, monkeys, and small deer. They also steal the food of other animals whenever possible. Like leopards, these shy cats are excellent climbers and generally hunt at night.

The African golden cat begins to mate when it is 2 years old. About 1½ months after mating, the female gives birth to a litter of one to three kittens. The kittens nurse for 3 or 4 months, and then begin to eat meat. Adults can live up to 12 years in captivity.

THE AFRICAN WILDCAT

African wildcats are the ancestors of modern house cats. The ancient Egyptians were the first people to keep African wildcats as pets, and cats played an important role in their society. They were considered sacred and may have been sacrificed to win the approval of gods. Modern *archeologists* have discovered a 4,000-year-old Egyptian tomb that contained seventeen mummified cats along with their pots of milk.

The African wildcat looks a lot like the domestic cats we keep today. It is stocky and weighs up to 18 pounds (8 kg). It is about 16 inches (41 cm) tall and 46 inches (117 cm) long. Its coat is striped and may be brown, gray, or yellow.

Although this cat lives only in Africa, it has close relatives in Europe, Asia, and the Middle East. Like the African golden cat, the African wildcat hunts mainly at

The African wildcat is the ancestor of all modern house cats.
These cats were worshipped by the ancient Egyptians.

night and is a skilled climber. It preys on rodents, birds, lizards, fish, frogs, spiders, scorpions, insects, and snakes.

The female begins mating when she is about 9 months old, while the male takes about 22 months to mature. About 2 months after mating, a litter of up to five kittens is born. Some females have two litters in a single year.

The kittens begin hunting when they are about 3 months old, and leave their mothers after about 5 months. They may live as long as 15 years in captivity.

THE BLACK-FOOTED CAT
The black-footed cat has a sandy-colored coat with round dark spots that often blend together to form

rings. It is the smallest African cat—and one of the smallest cats in the world. The black-footed cat weighs as little as 2.2 pounds (1 kg). It is about 10 inches (25.4 cm) tall and 22 inches (56 cm) long. Despite their size, these little cats make a lot of noise.

Black-footed cats live in hot, dry regions of southern Africa. To avoid the heat, they hunt at night. In some cases, they cover up to 5 miles (8 km) a night looking for food. They are also called anthill tigers because they

The black-footed cat is the smallest African cat. It hunts at night, and rests in termite mounds during the day.

rest in cool termite mounds or aardvark burrows during the heat of the day. These cats are known to sleep for up to 20 hours in a 24-hour period.

Unlike most other cats, black-footed cats are excellent diggers. They often use this skill to capture small animals. Like many other cats, they kill their prey with a neck bite. They get most of their water from their food, which includes rodents, hares, insects, reptiles, birds, eggs, and spiders.

Black-footed cats mate when they are 1 to 1½ years old. One or two kittens are born about 2 months after mating. If the mother cat senses danger, she warns her kittens to run or hide by making a series of special sounds. When the danger has passed, she calls them back with a series of soft sounds. Adult cats use loud meows to communicate with each other.

THE JUNGLE CAT

Jungle cats have slender bodies with long legs, a narrow face, large tufted ears, and a short tail with a black tip. Their fur is brown, gray, or red. These cats weigh up to 30 pounds (13.5 kg), stand about 16 inches (41 cm) tall, and are 48 inches (122 cm) long.

Thousands of years ago, jungle cats were kept as pets by the ancient Egyptians. Like African wildcats, jungle cats were sometimes mummified and placed in tombs. Some archeologists think that Egypt's Great Sphinx

Jungle cats were kept as pets by ancient Egyptians.
Their long legs make them excellent runners.

statue may have been modeled after a resting jungle cat. Today, jungle cats live in forests or grasslands, as well as on farmland in North Africa, Asia, and Sri Lanka. They are often found near streams.

These cats prefer to hunt during the day. They are excellent swimmers and jumpers, and use these skills to catch birds, rodents, amphibians, lizards, fish, and insects. Their long legs also help them capture prey.

Jungle cats begin to mate when they are about 1½ years old. About 2 months after mating, females give birth to as many as six kittens. The kittens nurse for about 5 months. By that time, they can hunt well enough to feed themselves.

THE SAND CAT

Sand cats have big ears on the sides of their heads and thick, sandy-colored fur. They weigh up to 8 pounds (3.6 kg), stand about 12 inches (30.5 cm) tall, and are 36 inches (91 cm) long.

This cat lives in the deserts of Asia, the Middle East, and Africa's northern Sahara region. To avoid the hot sun, the sand cat hunts at night and spends the day in its cool burrow. Its thick fur helps insulate its body during the heat of the day and the cold of the night. Thick black fur on the bottom of its feet protects the cat from the burning sand. When a sand cat gets too hot, it can lose heat through the thin skin on its ears.

Sand cats depend on their keen sense of hearing while hunting prey, such as birds, reptiles, insects, snakes, jerboas, and hares. These animals provide the cats with all the food and water they need. When a sand cat has eaten its fill, it covers the kill with sand and saves it for next time it feels hungry. Like black-footed cats, sand cats are excellent diggers.

Sand cats begin to mate when they are about 10 months old. To find a mate, these cats bark loudly at night. Humans often mistake the sand cat's bark for that of a dog. Females give birth to kittens about 2 months after mating. A typical litter consists of one to five kittens. Young sand cats drink their mother's milk until they are about 5 weeks old. They begin to hunt for themselves when they are 3 or 4 months old. In captivity, sand cats may survive for up to 13 years.

Sand cats live in the desert. At night, they sometimes make sounds like a barking dog.

Chapter 7

PROTECTING THE AFRICAN CATS

Most African cats are threatened, endangered, or near extinction. As human populations expand, cats lose their habitat and their food supply. Some begin killing livestock, and are then hunted and killed by farmers. When human populations are close, a few big cats turn into man-eaters. But often man-eaters are only cats that can no longer hunt their natural prey.

Although many African cats are protected by laws and international agreements, such as the Convention in International Trade in Endangered Species (CITES), *poaching* continues. While more than 100 countries have adopted CITES, cats are still being killed for their fur and as a source of food. In some regions, people also use cats' body parts to make folk remedies.

Many of the existing African cat populations are small. For the most part, these animals are protected only within the borders of a national park. Parks use *eco-tourism* to support their costs. Unfortunately, some cat populations in parks are threatened by disease. For example, many cheetahs in Serengeti National Park are infected with feline immunodeficiency virus (FIV).

FRICAN CAT POPULATIONS IN THE WILD

rican Cat	Estimated Population	Where They Live
on	Africa: 50,000 India: 250–300	Botswana, Kenya, Namibia, South Africa, Zimbabwe; protected over most of its range; also India
eopard	200,000–350,000	Ivory Coast, South Africa, Tanzania, Zaire, Zimbabwe;protected over most of its range; also India, Middle East, Borneo, Java, Sumatra, Malaysia
heetah	10,000–20,000	Ethiopia, Kenya, South Africa; protected over most of its range; may also be found in Iran
aracal	Unknown	Namibia, South Africa; throughout central Africa, not protected over most of its range; also Middle East, Asia, India
erval	Unknown	Found throughout most of Africa, except far north and south; not protected over most of its range
rican lden cat	Unknown; perhaps less than 50,000	Western and central Africa, Uganda, Ivory Coast; protected in a number of countries
rican ldcat	Unknown	Widespread, but breeding with house cats has decreased number of pure wildcats; not protected over most of its range
ack-footed t	Unknown; rare	Common in parts of Botswana and South Africa; *species* protected over most of its range; also in Middle East
ngle cat	Unknown; but fairly common	Northern Africa, Egypt; not protected over most of its range; also Asia, Europe
nd cat	Unknown; small population	Desert regions of northern Africa; not protected over most of its range; also Asia, Middle East

Many lions in the same park have been infected with a canine distemper virus. Both of these viruses come from domesticated pets.

Because many small wild cats *interbreed* with feral (wild) domestic cats, wildcat populations are growing small in their natural habitat. Fortunately, a number of parks and zoos are breeding large and small wild cats as well as cheetahs and releasing them into their natural environment. Scientists hope this practice will keep wild cat populations healthy and strong.

While these efforts are helpful, they are not enough to guarantee the survival of the African cats. These animals need a place to live and grow. All the nations that contain these cats' natural environments must set aside enough land to protect and preserve wildlife populations. Humans have the ability to either save or destroy the African cats. Their future is in our hands.

GLOSSARY

ANCESTOR—the ancient creature from which a modern plant or animal descended. Some scientists believe that dinictis is the ancestor of all modern cats.

ARCHEOLOGIST—a researcher who studies ancient cultures by examining their artifacts.

ARID—dry areas, like deserts, with 10 inches (25.4 cm) or less of yearly rainfall.

CANINE—one of the large front "fangs" of an animal, also called an eyetooth.

CARNASSIAL—a side tooth used by carnivores to shear chunks of meat off a victim.

CARNIVORE—an animal that eats only meat.

CAPTIVITY—being held in a zoo or some other unnatural setting.

COALITION—a group of male cheetahs that lives and hunts together.

DEWCLAW—the first claw on a cat's front paws. It is

useless in most cats, but cheetahs sometimes use it to trip prey.

DIGITIGRADE—animals that walk on their toes, with their heels raised off the ground.

ECOTOURISM—a business that uses tourist money to support the environment.

HYOID BONE—a bone that connects the tongue to the skull.

INTERBREED—to mate with a closely related species and produce young that are healthy, except that they cannot bear young of their own.

JERBOA—a jumping rodent with long hind legs and a tail.

MIACID—the animal from which all carnivores descended.

NOMADIC—an animal that roams over a large area.

ORIENT—to put in the correct position.

PAPILLAE—small hooklike projection on a cat's tongue that are used to remove meat from a victim.

POACHING—illegal trapping or killing of animals in order to obtain their fur, body parts, or as pets.

PREY—an animal killed for food by another animal (a predator).

PRIDE—a group of lions that live and hunt together.

POLYGAMOUS—an animal having more than one mate.

RETRACTILE—capable of being pulled back (into the claw).

SCAVENGER—an animal that eats dead animals that it did not kill.

SEMIDESERT—a dry area that has many characteristics of a desert, but receives more rainfall than a true desert.

SPECIES—a group of animals that look alike and can reproduce only with each other.

SUPERSTITION—an incorrect belief that results from ignorance, fear of the unknown, or trust in magic or chance.

TAPETUM LUCIDUM—a group of cells that reflect the light that enters the retina.

UNGULATE—hoofed animals, mainly herbivores that are horned.

VOMERONASAL ORGAN—an area on the roof of a cat's mouth. It allows the animal to record scents as it inhales.

RESOURCES

BOOKS

Arnold, Caroline. *Lion.* New York: Morrow Junior Books, 1995.

Esbensen, Barbara, J. *Swift as the Wind: The Cheetah.* New York: Orchard Books, 1996.

Lumpkin, Susan. *Small Cats.* New York: Facts on File, Inc., 1993.

Ryden, Hope. *Your Cat's Wild Cousins.* New York: Dutton, 1991.

Scott, Jonathan. *The Leopard Family Book.* Saxonville: Picture Book Studio, 1991.

CD-ROMS

African Wildlife. Gazelle Technologies, 1992.

Dictionary of the Living World. Compton's Learning Company, 1993.

Multimedia Animals Encyclopedia. Applied Optical Media Corporation, 1992.

The San Diego Zoo Presents . . . The Animals! Software Toolworks, 1993.

Wild Africa: Serengeti, Ngorongoro, and Tarangire. Sumeria, Inc., 1995.

Zoo Guides: Mammals of Africa. REMedia, 1993.

ORGANIZATIONS

African Wildlife Foundation
1717 Massachusetts Avenue, NW
Washington, DC 20036
TEL: (202) 265-8393
FAX: (202) 265-2361
Website: http://www.awf.org

American Zoo and Aquarium Association (AZA)
Office of Membership Services
Oglebay Park
Wheeling, West Virginia 26003
TEL: (304) 242-2160
FAX: (304) 242-2283
Website: http://www.aza.org

International Society for Endangered Cats of Canada, Inc.
124 Lynnbrook Road S.E.
Calgary, Alberta T2C 1S6
TEL: (403) 279-5892
Website: http://www.cadvision.com/iseccan

World Wildlife Fund
1250 24th Street NW, Suite 400
Washington, DC 20037
TEL: (202) 293-4800
FAX: (202) 775-8287
Website: http://www.wwf.org

INDEX

ABOUT THE AUTHOR

Geoffrey C. Saign loves to sail, dive on reefs, and hike in forests. He has a background in wildlife biology and has assisted in field research on a number of animals including hummingbirds and humpback whales. *The African Cats* is Mr. Saign's second book for Franklin Watts. He is also the author of *The Great Apes* (Franklin Watts, 1998) and the nationally endorsed *Green Essentials: What You Need to Know About the Environment* (Mercury House, 1994). Mr. Saign has spent the last decade counseling disadvantaged children and adolescents. He currently resides in St. Paul, Minnesota.